The Mothers

by

Erika Eckart

Finishing Line Press
Georgetown, Kentucky

The Mothers

Copyright © 2025 by Erika Eckart
ISBN 979-8-89990-261-1 First Edition
All rights reserved under International and Pan-American Copyright Conventions. No part of this book may be reproduced in any manner whatsoever without written permission from the publisher, except in the case of brief quotations embodied in critical articles and reviews.

Publisher: Leah Huete de Maines
Editor: Christen Kincaid
Cover Art: Cheng Wei via Shutterstock
Author Photo: Erika Eckart
Cover Design: Erika Eckart

Order online: www.finishinglinepress.com
also available on amazon.com

Author inquiries and mail orders:
Finishing Line Press
PO Box 1626
Georgetown, Kentucky 40324
USA

Contents

Attachment parenting
    I. Mycelium 1
    II. Bonds 2
    III. Tethered 3
The Mothers 4
Unraveling 5
As you run out of viable eggs 6
Offerings
    I. Kin-dling 7
    II. Natural Causes 8
    III. How to make a break in the canopy 9
Teeth 10
Cost Benefit Analysis 11
Gluttony 12
Genesis
    I. In the beginning there was only sea 13
    II. A part/apart 14
    III. Pull 15
    IV. Custard or the conservation of mass 16
Surrogate 17
Never let me go 18
Cry it out 19
The disappearing mothers of Victorian baby photography 20
Sacrament 21
You may wonder where the tenderness is 22
Adaptive Parenting
    I. Changeling 23
    II. The Pull of the Water 24
    III. Bargain 25
    IV. Ladies and Gentleman 26
    V. Multiverse 27

The Bends
    I. Short Shorts 28
    II. Persephone 29
    III. The Bends 30
When you cannot release your young
    I. Our baby was born without skin 31
    II. Empty Nest 32
    II. Thank the Phoenicians 33
Containment 34
Infestation 35
Adaptation 36
Plagues 37
Fairy Tales 38
Boogieman 39
Branches 40
Grandmother 41
Into the woods
    I. I can explain 42
    II. An oven, a high tower, a wolf's stomach 43
    III. Archetypes 44
    IV. What hunger makes you do 45
    V. Fattened up 46
Tapestry 47
Like Demeter 48
Cut 49
ROI 50
Prepper 51
Fruitful 52
Sight 53
Plenty 54

*For Mark, Ella, Archer, and Alice for making life worth writing about.
And for my forever muse, my late and desperately missed mother, Angel.*

Attachment Parenting

I. Mycelium

I'm told I must draw a line, but I can't figure out where I end and my children begin—like the mint in the garden that jams its appendages in the ground, travels sideways, sprouts up feet away, clear across the lawn. You'd never know it shares a body, but when you pull, it unravels in unexpected places. And even though roots do not fix us together, when they wilt, I wilt. I feel vindicated lately because there is new debate on whether there is a line at all. They found an aspen forest that breathes as one, all the trees turn lemon yellow in the fall simultaneously, every individual merely a limb on a larger body. Likewise, because mushrooms grow on top of their ancestors, what makes an individual is hard to say. When you cut one from its loam, it disrupts all. A peek below the soil reveals the reason: the mycelium, a chalky web connecting them, a system of disorganized diagonals, like a map of rivers, or the paths of the stars when you connect their dots. Doctors struggle to cure our fungal infections (the mushrooms that bloom in us) because (having a recent common ancestor) in taking down the fungus, we poison ourselves. Maybe this is because we have it too: a subterranean webbing, roots darting under the soil, pulsing with whispered secrets across time. Our mycelium, like a web of stars, a highway system, a blanket of life, is woven so tightly there is no way to say where each of the threads starts or ends.

II. Bonds

When I was eight, my great-grandmother told me to be her eyes. The trouble was we were decaying at different rates. As she tracked my height in the door jamb her hand grew less and less steady. And I sensed doom when I found her struggling to make the five steps from the bedroom to the bathroom, or in a reverie clipping nothing from the paper, making stacks of it, putting it in envelopes marked with a date in the future because who knows, I might need them. I clutched these envelopes, hid them in my underwear drawer, partly because I didn't want anyone to know how bad it had gotten, but partly because maybe she was right: when she is gone, I will need them. I will hold them, try to feel their current, use the little bit of charge left in them, to keep me going, my outer layer stable.

III. Tethered

On the news, the aerial panning shot of the beach coated with whale bodies reads like an ancient inscription, the scattered hatch marks of their remains are characters in a forgotten language, tea leaves telling us something. The reporter describes the smell: overwhelming, a million rancid fish markets, thousands of pounds of bodies about to explode with rot if someone doesn't do something soon. No one knows why seemingly healthy whales beach themselves. It might be navy sonar or some quirk in the shape of the ocean floor that makes them do it, sure, but there is a theory that they are so tightly bonded when faced with loss they commit mass suicide. This is predicated on other shows of attachment: sometimes adult males follow their mothers in death for no reason but heartbreak, and when a captive whale had her baby taken away, she rammed herself against the side of the tank, cried out with vocalizations no human had ever heard, long distance wails at lower frequencies, the kind that travel farther in the deep ocean—having never lived in the wild, never having heard these sounds, somehow she found them, in the rubbery gray folds of her brain, the clicks and screeches that would locate the lost little one if only there were sea between them instead of sky. So maybe, scientists think, when one is sick and in resignation dawdles in the short water where you can feel and see the sun, they all follow. Maybe they're confused, maybe begging the ill member to return with them to the deep sea, but maybe they know their mother/daughter/cousin is done for and they've decided they can't go on, that life after is too dim. That to wade into the shallows and let the tide take them away is better than a lifetime of calling out to their missing member and receiving only silence in return. Maybe that's the message the beached bodies leave us: a tether works two ways, it can keep you safe and attached or pull you under. It all depends on buoyancy, the weight of the object, and the size of the waves.

The Mothers

Like the young that crawl from their eggs and eat their mother's corpse for their first meal, this is our great dream: that our old dry bodies will flake away and amass and the pile will convert magically to pliant, rosy, new skin. We throw little pieces of ourselves on the pile out back where we burn the garbage: clumps of hair, loose teeth, swathes of skin with a little meat underneath. In this way we make the ash, the fertilizer, the rich compost, damp and red-brown and vegetal, to nourish our offspring. Morning glories do this, use their spent bodies to support their just sprouted seeds. Their dried remains become the scaffolding for the young to climb until the tendrils can support themselves and choke their ancestors into a dust nobody notices. Perhaps it happens in the night or in such small quantities nobody sees, because one day those old gray vines are gone and flowers have sprung where they once were.

Unraveling

Tell me the story again, about her ovaries like dried cereal. Useless rocks in sacks. She tried so hard: hormones, extraction, prayer, but she remained as barren as the desert. She lay very still while they injected her with her husband's semen, and then that of a stranger, after she'd been abandoned for a wide-hipped woman. She even had a phantom of all the wished-for babies, missed real periods, swelled, but it was just air and want, and the doctors said it would retreat in time. I heard she took to her basement, making porcelain and gray clay figurines which she put on display in the curio cabinet where her children's photos and bronzed booties should have been. She painted overalls on elephants, pigtails on small girls with heart lips, eyelashes on baby cubs, made an intentional mistake on each, so as to not outshine God. Well what's the difference, she'd said to no one in particular, I made them with my own two hands? Once in a magazine, she saw three crocheted old women unraveling yarn from their own legs to create crocheted babies and thought, *that is the motherhood I've always wanted: to be subsumed, to create something new and beautiful from my old parts while I still can.*

As you run out of viable eggs

you envy all the pre-pill women, who had no choice and by now might be nearly grandmothers, with no needling feeling that they took the wrong path. They were like monarch butterflies, who travel a thousand-mile loop over four generations because a sensor reading the signals of light and temperature orders them to deposit eggs at a preset distance from their predecessor. And even though their parents are dust, caterpillars emerge, who become butterflies and make the next leg of the journey. A closed circle, a white elephant gift tossed back and forth for infinity, acting on their programming, ensuring the survival of the fire-and-soot-colored creatures—never having to wonder if they should.

Offerings

I. Kin-dling

In the animal kingdom, some species use a surplus strategy: ants, fish, coral. They spew tens of thousands of tiny pearls of possible life to play the numbers, acknowledging that only enough survive to make the next link in the chain. The others become food, scaffolding, carbon. One out of 100,000 will emerge, crawl over its sibling corpses, stand on their shoulders, ribcages, legs, tentacles to make its way, to make everybody's way. When in protest monks drench themselves in gasoline and light a match, is it the same instinct? They present their limbs, face, torso as fuel to sustain others. Is that how they stand completely still as their robes (already fire-colored, now aglow) dance, whipping into the sky, trying to free the body, to offer it to something bigger, praying it will accept?

II. Natural Causes

Once they reproduce, mother octopuses never eat again. They hover over their thousands of eggs, glistening like gelatinous jewels, and stay stone still, for months, ever alert, growing less and less voluminous. Why do they starve to brood, to breed? Egg guarding is a full-time job, defenseless and delicious as eggs are, but even handed an already lifeless fish, mother Octopi reject it. In captivity, scientists turned the hunger strike button off and female octopuses lived long lives after they have copied themselves, occupied the same tank as their descendants, finally dying of old age. This intentional wasting isn't essential, just an efficient adaptation: what use could they be after fulfilling their duty? Already shapeshifters, muscles that can make themselves into anything, they gradually convert to flaccid goo, and then, finally, are torn apart by the same predators they eluded pre-maternity. Sharks are messy eaters so little bits of the mother octopuses' bodies fall like slow-motion snow. A meal for whatever is waiting with an open mouth. Often, the mothers are dead before their eggs hatch, but sometimes the barely visible newborns glide past the mother's body shrapnel, baby and mother the same size now, identical to the naked eye, but for the way they are moving in opposite directions.

III. How to make a break in the canopy

Pull from an almost empty reservoir, scratch your nails into the sides, claw to get any last bits. Then, refill it from nothing, a magic trick like a quarter from behind the ear. You see, you will have to make weather, pull the moisture from the sky, and in the end, you will be drained, spent, a time-lapse photography version of a tree, in the final frames being digested by fungi, microorganisms, your hollow shell a habitat. But, nearby a seedling will have taken root against the odds, will nurse off the organic matter the rain leaches from your body, will take advantage of the break in the canopy you have left, and rise toward the light.

Teeth

Hardly attached, they tumble from your mouth, and you hold them until you find a bathroom to check the damage. While you inspect the bits of bloody porcelain, and confirm these are indeed your teeth, you are reminded how your babies leeched your bones to make theirs, how they hollowed you out, left you calcium-less and crumbling. You wonder if maybe this is why some mothers turn to eating clay, when they're hungry, famished, really. Filled with an insatiable longing, they eat and eat, gorge, but are somehow still empty. From these meals, they refashion the teeth, hip sockets, lost hair (using the spaghetti attachment), occasionally a vagina or abdomen, cracked under the strain. But in the kiln, things do not go as expected, cracks appear, sometimes a rebuilt bone is too thin and collapses. The replacements are close to the real thing but off, the tough overworked ends of dough piled together, oversaturated by flour, the glutens too far gone; whatever you make out of them now might be functional but it won't be pretty. But still, they feed, chewing on the one good side of their mouth, try to replenish themselves. They smile with mouths closed concealing the teeth, still darkened in spots despite their efforts.

Cost Benefit Analysis

There is something left, a few seeds in the bottom of the bag, you hate to throw out; it is raw material whether you need it or not. It would be gluttonous, but you feel you should eat it. You will be bloated, but there will be no regret that you left some worthwhile thing for the trash. It's about frugality, home economics, like the last little nub at the back of the fridge, wrapped up in styrofoam that will never biodegrade, but you brought it home because you couldn't bear to see it go to waste. There is the simple cost benefit analysis, daycare and diapers, yes, but it doesn't consider the intangibles, the dearest currency of all: the cheek brushed against yours, the soft body wanting to be in your orbit and you wanting so badly to be in theirs, and how the gravity between those celestial bodies is what keeps us all from spinning out of control.

Gluttony

In fairy tales, the wicked eat the children, and not subtly either: they smack their lips with anticipation, prepare the darlings carefully by basting the tiny bodies and putting apples in their tiny child mouths. You hear it all the time when an aunt grabs a fat thigh between her thumb and forefinger and with a smile threatens to devour, to eat them up. And in small ways we do eat our young, feed off their stores, metabolize their still dewy flesh, swallow little rations of hope by watching them filter sand through their fingers for the first time, be first touched by a wave, feast on their look of conquest when they scale the wall of their crib. Sometimes you put more on our plate than you need or deserve or should have, because you are insatiable. Is it gluttonous to enlarge the land your cooled magma takes up, to want more voices to fill the chamber of our dimmed room on Christmas eve, to want to be surrounded by life when you've already had so much? And you live in a world where icebergs are cleaving into the ocean, and when she is 40, you might be dead, and you have already blown into a child's sweaty hair as they slept on your chest, how dare you ask for more? You should be reasonable, let the water wash over you, push the plate away, and say you've had your fill. But with sea level rise, and hungry people everywhere, is there any other choice than to beg another serving, add more land even though you know someday the ocean will come for it and lap its sides too?

Genesis

I. In the beginning there was only sea

There was no ground, only ebbing waves in all directions. All of the oxygen, matter, calories were consumed, spent, spread thin like the last bit of butter stretched over the surface of a saltine to be enough to quiet your hunger. And when you make it out and look back there is no linear time, all of it piled together, unsorted, bleary, like oil on a lens. No, I remember now, there was the first bit of land: a squirming body moving in your direction, pulling for you, satiated by you, and there was, like in the origin stories, a volcanic explosion forming that first bit, an initial burst of blood and sticky water clinging to their skin, their eyes sealed most of the time and when open you gazed at them as if entranced, and it was your sole duty to add earth to the island, to grow it imperceptibly through smaller explosions, each layer painful because your breasts turned to a green-blue iridescence, balloon sculptures gone wrong, and when loosed from the pressure bandage the ache was destabilizing, a pulsing radiation making you moan and leak plump tears, which left dark spots on the baby below who couldn't help themself but do their part to amass more territory and bite down.

II. A part/apart

Have you ever seen a baby root? This is when like pigs pushing their snouts around in the muck, they thrust their heads from side to side, their mouths in an anticipatory-O, looking for their mother's breast, and when they hit anything that protrudes the least bit, they push their heads forward with a surprising force and start suckling. If they latch to a non-milk providing nub, they cry out, throw their bodies slack, bicycle their legs, betrayed. This is what my daughter does to someone else while I reinforce the importance of aligning subjects with verbs. At lunchtime in the bathroom, I try to extract what she is looking for, and at first, it bursts forth, milky streams in all directions, so much pressure, but after a few minutes it slows to a trickle and the bottles don't seem to be filling at all, and there is a fear that I won't even be able to give her this, that I've told myself is a proxy, something of me while I'm gone, the least I can do. But making milk is not just mechanical, it's your body responding to the child begging before you, your skin on theirs, triggering the release of the precious fluid. So I imagine we are yearning for each other at the same moment: her furious body, her soft cheek, the way she pins me down with her foot, my curled up abdomen cradling a breast pump disguised as a work bag instead of a child, trying to bridge the space between us, to bend space time, to be together, to eke out a few more drops to bring home to her.

III. Pull

A new mother died of ebola and her tiny baby was left in a box, cardboard, not to be held until the waiting period expired, but the baby tested negative and the nurses couldn't resist comforting the motherless child, pressing it against them and cooing and rocking in that instinctive way, (we all know it; our hips move in that same rhythmic dance long after our babies are grown, like sailors whose bodies never quite return to land) and the baby, quieted, slept and everything was happy and normal and this was something you can control. Except the baby didn't make it. 12 of the 13 nurses died, too. Every time I remember that my son is swaddled elsewhere in someone else's arms, not mine, milk seeps from my breasts, an ancient ache, a second set of tear ducts. By midday, all my shirts have hardened circles, stiff ghost areolas, despite the absorbent pads, my body manages to scrawl a message: please, it begs, please, just let me hold him.

IV. Custard

It is a relief to be emptied, to be suckled from, to be a fat store, to be transformed into a more beautiful thing. And it is a clock, it is time, a metronome, an hourglass filling and then turned over. And when they fatten like a candle dipped in wax, a little day by day, it is your strangely-translucent milk that made it happen. Your baby is made of milk, their custard flesh enlarged by it and while it is the most obvious thing, you are so proud when the doctor weighs them and smiles, because you are tired and it did hurt even though it is what you are programmed to do, made to and all these mammals have managed it, and existence in some ways hinges on it, but, still you made this custard baby with your body, from nothing.

Surrogate

Deprived of parents, monkeys picked a simulated foam and terry cloth surrogate (even when blunt spikes poked out from it) over the wire and wood one bearing milk, because, of course, everyone wants something more than food. They nuzzled the imitation mother's soft surface for hours to make do and those deprived of first a real and then a soft dummy mother thrashed their heads against the sides of the cage. To replace myself for 10 hours a day, simulate my soft body, I diced, boiled and pureed, made hyper-colored yam, berry, carrot ice cubes, set a rotation, in between the plastic bladders of scrambled-egg-colored milk which I squeezed from my body. Then, when teeth pierced your gums, I left you maraschino-cherry-eyed pancakes, halved grapes, crust-less triangles. Mostly you left them uneaten, flies circling, color changing as the moisture evaporated and the morsels turned to foam bricks. But, I piled the fresh on the rotten, making stratified layers: vibrant cantaloupe and pineapple arranged in a smiley face, transition to a murky gray stew spotted with spores of chartreuse, forest, lime. More than food they are tribute, piled up outside your altar, a compost pile of what good mothers do. An incantation, a prayer, a pleading: "*Look what I made you.*" Sitting there like a dummy, all mother-shaped and rotting.

Never let me go

Once upon a time, it was just my tiny baby and me. She was trapped in a time loop of puking and then heaving with nothing left to come out, just bursts of silence. Then, exhausted, she slept like a cursed princess: pearlescent, frozen, terrifying. She was so still, I put my finger under her nostrils to feel her small, warm breath. I worried she'd wilt in my hands. I called the doctor. He had me check her color, keep track of the last time she peed. She'll be fine, he said, get some rest. I'd nod off for a few minutes and then wake, startle into manic alert, scared I had left my post for too long. I went to splash some water on myself, and saw my face in the mirror: skin marbled with milkglassblue veins, hair in the lumpy pony tail of the unshowered. So I was weak when the documentary came on about how bonobos share traits like grief with us. In it, a mother cradled her dead baby for weeks. There was a time-lapse montage as the baby started to decompose. It must be hot where they were because by the end she was caressing bone with overcooked-chicken skin: crispy, suspended like moth wings. The narrator wondered why she continues to carry it, suggesting it might be because the mummification has frozen it in baby shape. Maybe, I thought, they aren't only like us in their love for their young, their romantic jealousies and their petty theft, maybe they have stories too, and perhaps like me this mother in her grief-fever imagined this was a spell brought upon by an evil queen for some small error she made long ago. If she just loved her little one hard enough, she could bring her back.

Cry it out

When my great grandmother was a child, her parents would slice up an apple between 7 siblings, so when her children and much later I arrived in times of plenty she fed us until our skin stretched, striped iridescent from the pressure, until once until I vomited out the car window. She would have us know fullness to make up for all her want. Each meal was several courses, even in the middle of the night, I was served a lavender melamine bowl of peaches, pound cake, a foot-long hot dog, an iceberg salad drenched in orange dressing, chicken soup. I'd catch her watching me eat, smiling. So maybe having been separated from my mother until I was 7 I couldn't resist lavishing my baby with touch, couldn't let my dear one cry it out alone reaching out and finding no one there. I tried the way of the books: nursed her until the milk dribbled down her face, put her down, waited down the hall, ignored the screams. But it was no use. She scaled the sides of the crib, threw her small body against the door. So I begged forgiveness, let her curl against me like a snail nestles a ship, but now she is cursed to be awake unless rocked to sleep or pushed in a stroller to a particular mixtape. She can't "self-soothe" and they warn this has consequences. For every night I had gone to sleep unheld, away from my mother, for how I had learned to wrap a blanket tightly around my shoulder like a Cocoon to simulate the pressure of a person, I would cradle my little one twice as hard, babybook be damned, even though I know you can have too much of a good thing.

The disappearing mothers of victorian baby photography

They blend in, scaffolding the still wobbly child in the foreground who despite their efforts is a little blurry, unable to stay still the length of time the shutter needs to capture the light. An aura of movement glows around the babies' downy heads. Like the glow coming off infant jesus. Like a visual stutter. With their layered dresses and glassy eyes, they are enchanting, so you might not notice the mound of human topography behind them unless someone tells you and then you can't stop seeing them, cheap ghost costumes the wrong color with no eyes cut out. Mother-shaped masses of fabric, their phantom hands occasionally protruding. If they paid the man to expose the film with a flash that left the air saltpeter heavy, to watch the image paint itself in the chemicals, even added the upcharge to tint the sepia cheeks pink, dot the eyes with blue, why not just be in the photo uncloaked? Were they still paunchy or already heavy with the next one? No matter, now they are stilled forever in a phantom embrace, trying and failing to execute the impossible sleight of hand of motherhood that is caring for your children while disappearing. Their presence is more obvious especially to those of us with our own phantom arms, ghost thighs, residual limbs, we were unable to crop out, like in the one photo with Santa where my child is obviously terrified and I'm clutching him from the back desperate to make it look like this isn't all staged and crumbling, trying like always to make my scaffold invisible or at least inconspicuous, to create a fiction just long enough to capture the light.

Sacrament

When you listen to your sleeping children breathe, you sometimes reflexively cross yourself despite living most of your years away from the church door and the bowl of sacred water that sits by it which you would dip your fingers in and father son and holy ghost into an absolvent plus sign bathing you in grace. This is because the see-sawing of their rest is the thing most like the voices joined in song that filled the church's hull, made a body of sound rise up, like a seance. The collective was otherworldly, bright together concealing the individual weakness (off tune, hideous). The weight of this glorious sound blanketed you in an enchanted cloak, flawed threads woven into an impermeable knit. Like the magic paper cone that defies what you know about physics and holds water. It filled not just the body of the church, but your ribcage too, so much you might drown or really breathe for the first time, convinced you there might be a soul but that it is just one, like the sacrament we share it when we come together, and it is so bright you have to close your eyes to see it.

You may wonder where the tenderness is

you know, the motherhood of soft focus, billowing sheer fabric, and bosoms. Of coffee commercials, of a quiet christmas eve night, of enfolding. All you see here is the motherhood of the ominous empty playground swing still swaying, screeching car wheels, hand wringing, of *my dear, you'll need to sit down for this*. But these are love too, they are its relief, its negative. Tenderness is the light which casts this shadow. If you look closely, you can see it in its dark relief: in the quiet car tears, the caressing of a brow to check for heat, the looking for all the exits. It is my mother's and her mother's and her mother's, the dark sacrificial love of wearing the holey bleached t-shirt, of pretending you are not hungry even as you salivate, of lying down with a man who makes your stomach turn, so your children might have something, anything, you didn't have, of never saying how much you love them out loud, because the universe might hear you and take them away.

Adaptive Parenting

I. Changeling

In pre-industrial Europe, autistic children were thought to be fairy replacement children. Many were killed in the attempts to send them home to their fairy parents, who would come to retrieve their charge if abused enough.

Her mother had suspicions that she had been swapped, so had left her in the forest many nights hoping the fairies might come and take her back. Her mother said she couldn't take the icy gaze anymore, that she surely could not be hers. She was quite old the last time her mother tried, nearly seven, it was *probably no use at this age* she heard her whisper. That night tied to a tree, she feared some savage beast would eat her but something about the net of stars kept the wolves at bay. In the morning her mother returned, loosed her, gray with cold. The girl's gaze was still glassy, but the daughter was keen on what was happening and gave her mother a little smile, a nuzzle on the walk back knowing that is what she wanted, a reassurance that this one belonged to her. And she was saved. No more nights in the forest or meals in an eggshell. So when her child, just two, lost speech, seemed to be with them and then leave, like a plant that was about to blossom and is suddenly just a sprout again, and the elders, including her husband, ordered her to beat and burn him to summon his fairy parents, she faked it. The shovel she put him on was hardly warm, the switch hit to the ground instead of the boy's thighs; she told them this is definitely the real one now, but when he wrapped himself in a blanket and covered himself in hay and was nearly stabbed by a pitchfork, the father said he would do it himself this time. She overheard him with the elders, deciding if the oven or the river were a better means to rid them of this burden. *There is too much want in the world to be yoked by a fairy child*, they said. They must drive him out. As she rocked him, wrapped tightly as he liked, she thought *they know nothing about how much want there is in the world*. She recalled that night her mother left her, how she felt abandoned, yes, but also cradled by the forest. So she and the boy escaped into the thick of trees. They ate berries and nettle and what she could steal from farms in the night. She learned his language, and they tucked in corners of their small den of logs. After surviving a few winters keeping the predators at bay, the mother wondered if maybe they did have magical parents, and in their way, they had come for them both after all.

II. The pull of the water

He needs to throw himself in, to be the thing drug by the current and pulled under, to dance against the rocks. I anchor myself on the wet ground and hold him back; he wiggles. Everything is slick, the whole world a smooth, wet surface with no traction. It is impossible to create enough friction to keep upright, so I shift my weight and we fall back, away from the water, a panting, still-struggling pile. A stranger comes and asks *what are you going to do when he's too big for you?* My boy writhes on the wet ground; I'm pinning him, begging, explaining, promising, praying the stranger will walk away. It feels unsustainable, the pull of the forces, a seam about to burst somewhere in my mind or my stomach or the space time continuum. I start scream-singing "this little light of mine," scaring the stranger away and startling my boy out of his mania, and I remember hanging from the ceiling in the school cafeteria little paper mâché planets with signs explaining how long it will take their light to get to us, and how comforting it is to know someday it's coming, either the light or the current to carry us away.

III. Bargain

His mouth and eyes are in one plane and his legs and arms in another; it is time travel and dimensional change. Yesterday, when we tried to vaccinate him. Even though I was restraining him and he's only 9, he kicked two nurses down. One of them said mournfully "he's so strong," which normally with boys everyone says in the most fawning way. But no, she said it like it was a damn shame. Her downcast head shake said even more: if we don't get his behavior to match his size, then like an overinflated balloon he will be wrenched from our grasp, too powerful for us. Like the deal in Rumpelstiltskin, by the time the king got back this straw better be gold or else, that's how it is with him. He has to be made into something more prized by kings or they will take my baby. I'm reading fairy tales to learn the secrets of those mothers, how they kept the troll's maw from the feet of their babies. How they got to keep and cuddle their children undisturbed. It seems it is all about deals, cutting a good one. As I watch him on the floor of the 10 by 14 doctor's office all animal brain, terrified, hurting, kicking the wheeled stool in my direction, the rubber band of his spine arched as if 1,000 volts are moving through it, I wonder what bargains I can make, how can I trick the troll into looking the other way while we make our escape? I would give anything to keep him safe: my bones, my teeth, contracts for future babies, but my satchel is empty, all the en-magicked stones fell out when I wasn't looking. There is nothing I wouldn't trade for a door-less tower, or magic chalk, to draw a door here on this ancient oak, walk through to somewhere outside the king's dominion, to a secret village where he can grow as big as he pleases and we can stay together, always.

IV. Ladies and Gentlemen

As part of our show tonight, we invite you to ask a question. To prove it is not all rehearsed. As you see, there are no mirrors, no hidden speakers, no funny stuff. Just him speaking off the cuff. You there, what's your question? "Does he like ice cream?" you ask? So, son, do you? Uncomfortable pause. "icecreamyummyyes," he finally answers no spaces between the words, a wall of sound stitched together, a burst of light more than communication. Damp applause. I might even call it patronizing. *This is the part where you are supposed to gasp, folks—-our boy talks! No one thought it was ever possible! Marvel as he tells you his age, his grade, regales you with a story about construction worker clowns (I promise that's all him, folks. Who could come up with that?)!* We are only five minutes in, and we are both dripping in the heat of the spotlight, the top hats and bowties are stifling (is anyone else having a hard time breathing?) and our cheeks ache from our plastered smiles. Our jokes are shopworn, the stuff you find on popsicle sticks and the bored audience begins to heckle, screaming "What else have you got?" "Is that really all?" One disembodied voice in the back (I can't see who with the light in my eyes) yells: "Do you really think that is going to be enough?" The room gets quiet. I know they mean enough for him to drive a car, hold a partner's hand, live when I am dead. All at once, I see the meltdowns, the oncoming traffic, the faces screwed up against him everywhere. *I'm sorry, folks, it appears we are all out of time.* I cue the music, close the curtain, pray the giant cane pulls us to safety.

V. Multiverse

There are an infinite number of universes because they are always being born. In one of these universes you ride your bike alone in the forest, are kidnapped and they make a tv movie about it; I am the villain in this movie, not helicopter-y enough. In another, you were born a twin with a secret language all your own, so by the time you took Spanish you had three and, of course, the violin you started playing when you were a toddler, so four really. In a sixteenth, we are made of jam. Then there is one where you are the same, still you have trouble communicating and do the sometimes dangerous things, but the universe is ready for you, has bumpers on the edges of all the sharp corners, is filled with people who extend their hand to you and when I run out of ways to make our world match this one, I will engage in a physics experiment where I send an atom out again and again and while the atoms end where I can see them and we are still where we are, maybe somewhere I generated a version of the world ready to welcome you.

The Bends

I. Short Shorts

Do you think I'm fat? she asks me, the mirror, someone, anyone. She is contorted, Half a check is hanging out. The look on her face says she wants to collapse in, with great force like a cartoon-reenactment of the working of a black hole. I want it even now, the thing she is seeking, to collapse in on myself, to fold. Yes, to have long, angled limbs, but mostly that feeling of fingernails digging into my sides, creating a density that could cause implosion. I want to get smaller and smaller, to disappear, to be invisible, to be no bother, a wisp, a barely visible stroke with a calligraphy pen. It is an adaptation, these behaviors. It is the way we have survived in a world hostile to and hungry for our bodies. On some Polynesian Islands, birds have evolved to be flightless because of the lack of predators. Raspberry bushes there do not bother making thorns, because there is no one to eat them. What would it be to blossom in a place where there is nothing ready to devour us as soon as the first petal surfaces? Would we love our skin— grow it out—expand into available space, pliant and plushy, flaunting to each other the ability of our flesh to press back at fabric, to pull it apart at its seams?

II. Persephone

My insides rubbed raw and bleeding, my legs numb, and sure I could try to run away, but these are gods I am dealing with and squirming only makes it worse because like any predator they enjoy the fight. Now, below my feet, my girl, the flesh I made with mine and that I love better than my own, is being used against her will. It is one thing when they do it to you, it's another when they come for your babies. The only reasonable response is to kill everything, to wrench the chlorophyll from the leaves, to knowingly starve creatures who seem nice enough. It is the only way I can hope to save my girl from this shared fate, and how dare anything live, flourish, be verdant, dance on the grave of my baby? My other brother, the one who didn't take her, but who knew, condoned, allowed, and regularly takes gods and mortals for his pleasure, sometimes in disguise, tries to plead with me, *calm down, be reasonable*, calls me emotional, insists this is bad press because the starving are less obedient servants, says it is an affliction of my sex, this tendency to hysterics—when he and all like him are the real affliction. He stands before me, absurd, small, with the power only to destroy and not create, saying *let's make a deal, I'm sure we can work out some kind of arrangement, think about it from his perspective*. Starve, I scream, beg in the streets, you will not eat at my table again until my baby is returned to me.

III. The Bends

My girl chopped off all her hair. Before, I was tethered to the nightly ritual of detangling and braiding the thickets, which appeared each night at the base of her neck, sailor's knots, tangled by the wind and sweat and motion of her day. It was my job to find an entry point in each and, as gentle as possible restore order. Now, there will be no more dimly-lit nights wedged between my thighs of *stay still* and *beauty is pain*, no more of the tug, the chunks gripped, the tension of my pull and hers, her still warm from the bath and the room too hot really for sitting next to anyone. No more *How could you do this to me?* when my comb caught a difficult tangle. No more complaining about what I could do with this time, and *it would be so much easier if you could just be still*. So you would think I would be relieved it is over, but I just sit next to her anyway, stroke what is left of her hair until she is irritated, amble about picking up small things, bereft, unmoored. This is another way she doesn't need me anymore. These burdens, sloughing off a little at a time, are slowly shifting from me to her, the transition stair-stepped like methadone which is a kindness because if one day I awoke and this creature who so dearly depended on me and ate only from my body and clutched my fingers to fall asleep, whose cries were the tides that controlled my day all at once didn't need me anymore, I might float away from the sudden shock, an anchor cut from below. There's danger in letting go too quickly. Like how scuba divers cannot emerge from the pressure of great depths too fast, otherwise they will get the bends, pockets of air that bloom in their chests and explode. Instead, to surface safely they gradually reach little milestones, pulling back the compressing fingers of the water one at a time.

When you cannot release your young

I. Our baby was born without skin

so we must use a tiny brush to coat him in a film that keeps the water, dust, and sun mostly out, but bits of it get in the meat of his muscle, and we have to remove them with tweezers. The reapplication is nearly constant, when you finish the right toe, the left shoulder has nearly evaporated. We are reminded by events (the factory that made the product on which we depend burned down and we had to stay inside and use lightly oiled plastic wrap for a week) and passersby (*you know we can still see his heart beating, his massive lunch, you are not fooling anyone*) that this faux skin is temporary, marginal, suboptimal at best. We have tried for him to turn the tiny brush on himself, given detailed instructions, but there are so many parts he can't reach so without us the pharma skyn™ slips off, disgusting. a shriveled mass, more depressing than nothing, and he is left with his entrails and sinew exposed again. We are of course happy to do it, to take turns, to make a game out of the arduous process, to tap each other out for breaks, we enjoy it. I dream about it. My fingers have grown comfortable only in a brushing position, but we are staring into a darkness made of average life spans and subtraction. I've considered setting up a gofundme for a series of skin applicators to keep him cozy and closed for as long as possible. If that fails, we are trying at the very least to provide an umbrella, a raincoat, galoshes made of skin, to cover the most tender parts to not just have the flesh open to the wind.

II. When people complain to me about their empty nest

First, I must tell you, it is not an accurate metaphor for your ambling around noticing nobody has been here to muss anything up or leave the refrigerator open, for how it feels when your duty has been discharged, for how the pieces of you that live outside your body are beyond your reach now as you wait for their calls and take up building ships in bottles as a way to start a second act. You see, birds don't stay in their spent nests because they're plastered with bits of eggshell and feathers stuck on by white and black wads of birdshit. The detritus of baby-bird-making attracts mites and bacteria and predators. So, once the chicks fly on their own, they all sleep elsewhere: on the ground, tucked in a bush, sometimes still together mother and child, bunched up to stay warm. Second, as you bemoan to me the unsettling quiet in your house now, it is not the universal experience you think. Many of us will never empty our nests. My baby might not fly fully on his own why sleep in birdshit? We will, of course, have to abandon this thatch and straw sooner or later, the metaphor but also the birdshit, the soft under feathers, the bits of shell, but maybe we can make some new kind of home, together tucked behind a bush, in a grassy patch, bunched together, keeping warm taking care of each other until we can figure something else out.

III. Thank the Phoenicians

On the spaceship Earth ride at Epcot, Judie Dench explains how early man struggled to hunt food until the invention of spoken language which meant collaboration, meant flesh over a fire, then came written communication, then an alphabet (for which she asks us to thank the Phoenicians). Then, she describes the monks transcribing all known language, and finally the printing press, which she explains enabled all human knowledge to bloom, spread, transmiss. People would no longer have to build learning from scratch because writing gave us a baton to hand off and that is how we got to the computer, she says, and I remember that my mother has died since the last time we heard this voice through the speaker in the spaceship earth ride, and I think Judi Dench was still young-ish, maybe only 60 when she recorded this, and how the cutting-edge technology the screen before us is predicting will exist in the future (smart appliances!) is now butter-knife dull, and I wonder if the written words I transmit will create a fungible token of knowledge, a how-to kit for someone to make a better world, and maybe instead of poems I should be making something useful out of the gift of written language technology, like this strange gift Dench has left us, a guide for those that come after. So here goes nothing: when your child is disabled and you don't know how he will survive without you when you die, and your own mother has just died, my advice is as much as possible take him to the theme park and sit on the rides in the cool dark while he clutches your hand and asks "if the Phoenicians are like Aladdin" and say "close, similar, yes," and absorb that he couldn't do that last time you were here, nor answer because questions and connect schema, nor inquire about the animatronic Da Vinci painting the ceiling of the faux Sistine Chapel, all of which he is doing now. And when the ride uses an optical illusion to shoot you off into the twinkly future of the stars, and the screen asks him questions about how he will live in thirty years (will he have a place to live?) and what kind of job he will do (will he have any job at all?), and you start to choke up as you always do with these questions, remember how wrong we have always been, remember how Judi Dench promised us jetpacks, how language saved our species and how words might provide salvation even now as your son takes your hands from your face and is newly able to ask you what is the matter.

Containment

The problem is these waves are in you: long ago, forces were exerted, you were deserted, a child left to soothe a crying baby, to hide from the rental company in late afternoon shadows behind the very furniture they were there to reclaim, punched in the head over taking more rice krispies cereal than allotted. And now, that stored energy must have its equal and opposite reaction. The waves swell up to your throat and stop the passage of air. You try to hold them in, but they keep coming, drawn to the moon. You wonder how to subvert nature. How to not transfer that dark energy (from the pendulum of the steel-toed boot to the head or your mother's tears when she didn't have anything to feed you, or the laying low in the car so the cops won't know you are using it as a house) from your body of water to your child's. Despite your attempts at a calm sea, your focus on containment, the breathing exercises, you see the wave rise in your child too, a flinching, an apology when no wrong was done, an undercurrent threatening to become a riptide and you know it is already too late: as hard as you tried not to, you have already trickled into her estuary, filled it clear up, and set it in motion. Your dark water worms its way into everything—fills in the empty spaces, freezes and then expands, elbowing its way in, turning the cracks to chasms.

Infestation

We bleached the rug, but after a couple of days when I put my foot down they flurried again. Like memory, fleas are persistent: this one's parents may have existed long ago, stowed their eggs in the cracks of the hardwood, where they waited patiently for the pheromones of a host before hatching. What if this one is not alone? What if this invisible world has already ballooned, and thousands, millions, are affixing their colorless eggs on fibers of my sweater, are in the carpet under just below my daughter's sleeping head moving toward the smell of blood, shitting everywhere their pewter dust? Months later, I saw two lice in my daughter's hair. After crushing them, I couldn't find anymore, not even the pearlescent teardrop-shaped nits. Were they real or a flashback to being scared to look down at the crowns of my sisters' heads, at the web of life under their translucent strands, undulating, a forest in the breeze? Of fearing the school nurse would come in with her wooden stick and knit in my hair and send me out. Of my mother's face twisting under the unbearable cost. Maybe infestation is in my blood; I've passed it down. Like the dormant flea eggs, it never went anywhere, just waited for a host to emerge. A curse for escaping the studio apartment where roaches streamed up the drain to this sanitized suburban home. They're coming for me, reminding me this is where you came from, did you forget? Every night I make my children sit in my lap, section their hair with my pen, try to catch the light. I need to know they are uninhabited. I'm also hungry for the old pleasure of severing a nit's bond to the hair, the satisfaction of squeezing a louse between my thumb and forefinger and the red stain that means it is done for. Weeks pass of empty scalp, but in my dreams the lice squirm in an infinity loop, a disorganized school of fish, multiplying exponentially, becoming more and more covered until they are a solid block of pulsing black which follows me wherever I go because it all comes down to blood: being made from it, being thirsty for it.

Adaptation

You pass down suffering, no matter what you do—your DNA was bruised at the edges, mutated threadbare from one too many missed meals, too many impressions where a hand used to be on your upper arm, too many hours left unconsoled. Your genes take these secret messages about the past to the future, even when you burned the evidence, even when your girl's childhood is nothing like yours, there is no dumpster food from when the gas station caught on fire and everything had to be thrown out, all of it perfectly good, scurried into the apartment basement. Your daughter never relished a mesquite-flavored ding dong, such a pleasure for food to come at truly no cost, no wariness about whose mouth you are taking it from, no guilt about what someone will have to do to get more. Even when her childhood is full fruit bowls and "order whatever you want," your body scratched messages about scarcity and danger, baked into their bones the need to conserve, to flinch, to hide until it is quiet. Your girl puts back the more expensive yogurt at the store though no one told her to, though you always have stilled your face when the bill comes, hidden your habit of putting things back. She has inherited this adaptation like the bird that spends most of its time in the sky even though all its ground predators are long extinct. Still, it sleeps while airborne, half its brain resting at a time, in order to almost never land, to a stay above where they can even be perceived, to become almost one of the stars and in that way to avoid the trouble their very cells tell them is waiting for them if they dare to touch land.

Plagues

Sometimes the only way to love your child is to abandon her. Because you are lacking everything: laundry detergent, a place to wash clothes, a coat. And lacking even a river and thatched basket sealed with pith, the best you can do is to leave her on a porch and watch from the street to be sure someone opens the door. And periodically return to peek through the windows to make sure she's better off, but importantly remain unseen. It would be harder on her if she saw you. She needs a clean break, you tell yourself, to be left once is enough. But to be honest it would be harder on you too, to again cleave, to separate, because even now sometimes you feel the weight of her body still in the crook of your knee where you used to bounce her to sleep. And you see her stare. So aware. You could tell she knew what was going on, had already at three started asking questions— *Who is that man? Why are we sleeping here? What's wrong with you mom, you look different?* So you tell yourself you left her so she could have a better life, full of routine, warm beds, and meals, and eventually pre-school and kept your son because he was a year younger, barely weened, not old enough for the severing, but if you are being honest he was also not old enough to ask questions and seemed generally less inclined to notice the anomalies, content to curl up next to you wordlessly whenever he could, even in a strange apartment, on someone's couch, or in the backseat of a car you intermittently turn on, walking a delicate tightrope between dying from carbon monoxide and frostbite. And you promised her you'd be back for her in a few weeks, just until you get on your feet, and the woman who took her in greedily said take *your time, what is the rush* on the phone when you called to check, and you could hear your girl in the background, asking questions, *is that mama, when is she coming* and the woman, your own grandmother said *no, just a neighbor who borrowed some sugar—back to your nap*, and it stung like little cuts along your whole body splashed with alcohol, but your little girl sounded settled, like a child who could go back to her nap, so instead of rushing to her which is what the pain in your chest demanded, you stopped calling, stopped peeking in the window, better to cauterize the wound, burn the nerve endings, cleanse it with fire just like they do with the earth so something new can grow.

Fairy Tales

Was a woodsman going to come to save me? Was I to be restored to my rightful kingdom, having been missed all this time? Or was my Gradmother a savior, a salvager, nursing me with an almost-milk porridge that wasn't mother's but would nonetheless fatten me. She dipped me again and again, a wax child, almost identical to a one raised by its mother. And with each dip, with each day as no axman or mother arrived, I learned I was not stolen. No one was coming for me. She made me as best she could: a little misshapen, bangs at a diagonal, reeking of cabbage and ointments. She dressed me in anachronistic clothing brought from the eaves, like all the other children, but not. My play involved no mothering and no baby dolls, just action figures with pregnancy as a plot twist, divorces, betrayals, secret twins, just like in the stories my grandmother and I watched in the afternoons where I learned the word she used for my mother was an insult. I had a story, too: I was special. I was saved. I was left. When irritated, she reminded me of my story: not only was no one coming for me, but there was something terrible locked deep inside of me, under the milk and wax and hair and wool, deep down at the core. And so, I walked myself to school and put myself to sleep and wrapped the terribleness tight like a stone baby, knowing that real grandmothers could feed you and eat you, too.

Boogieman

I remember the cadaver-colored yellow-green of the linoleumed hallway, the day I sat a step below my mother who came for a rare visit to warn me about the Boogie Man. She was enormous, her strawberry blonde hair swinging out from a center part, Jordache jeans painted on her thighs, the effervescence of tic-tacs and snapping mint gum. It was on the news each half-hour, this man picking off little girls. I hadn't seen her in weeks, months, and I hung on her booming voice when she told me that Stranger Danger, when he inevitably arrived, would be middle-aged and moustached, with dirty fingernails sliding open a van door, to show me the glistening candy wrappers. He'd instruct me to "come here little girl." "Are you getting this?" she begged while she grabbed me at the thick of my upper arm with both hands, each finger leaving a mark. She taught me a secret password to use if I ever needed to and when she left an hour later, I whispered it like a mantra: "Cadillac, Cadillac, Cadillac." The words filled the air of the lizard-lit house, otherwise still and quiet, empty except for me and grandma now, all the windows and doors double-locked because you never know what's out there.

Branches

The girl on the radio talks about being left behind. Her parents had no choice, she says. She forgives, she says. But she can't help being angry and sad, even now reunited with them for a decade in the US. The girl says during one particularly rough patch in her adulthood, they took a photo of her brain which revealed blank spaces where the tendrils must have blinked, paused, too busy surviving to develop synapses. The doctor had told her a child abandoned by their parents develops a brain that looks like a tree without branches, nothing but a trunk reaching up for air. I wonder if mine is branchless too, gasping, or if it is like a wild oak, with gnarled grandmother's hands for branches, articulated, hinged, zigzagging, bent into whatever space is available, plunging earthward, before rising again, fingertips to the sky.

Grandmother

Once upon a time, I lived in her climate-controlled bungalow, where all of time collapsed like an archeologist's dream or nightmare. The combined hum of the television, radio, and humidifier sang a domestic lullaby. The air was sulphery with cabbage cooking and the churning in and out of 2 stomachs, always on the brink of too full. I never knew what it was to be hungry. She had lived through two world wars, a depression, I was her precious thing, an extra child. There was surplus now, more than we could ever need. She would make me know it. When fevered, she caressed my forehead; when well, she stroked my cheek. Every night, I slept in her bed, her comforting billows next to me. And her hacking cough into a million tissues. Each of them was carrying her out of the house, ounce by ounce until she was emptied of phlegm and gone. And I was expelled too, with a gnawing in my stomach I had never known, to my new home: a three-sided corrugated shack. There I was a burden, an extra mouth to feed, obviously a slut, *where are you going dressed like that?* On this path, obviously somewhere, I've a basket of nothing, a red cloak, inexplicably a corset and miniskirt. I'm going to find her, to find the feeling of being full again. And off I was. Hunger with its hands on my back. I searched under bridges, in thatched huts, in hollowed-out trees but just found grubs and dandelion greens, barely enough to fend off the stomach acid. Several times as I walked along the path, a wolf approached me. *Would you like to collect some flowers?* They'd ask, pulling me off my course. *Need a ride? Can we just talk?* Sensing danger in their grip, I wriggled away. *I should really get going. I've got someone waiting for me,* I lie. And somehow they knew it's not true. *You're so pretty, I want to be with you, I want to stay with you.* Their words dressed them like grandmothers, but they were clearly still wolves, teeth bared, tufts of fur at the ankles, wrists. *They do not mean what they say,* I remind myself, but their soft tones, the stroke of their hand across my brow made my mouth water. I squint to see what I'm hungry for: a comforting floral pattern, bosom, spectacles, her bed, the tissue box next to it. I'm interrupted by the wolf's banter: *You are delicious,* the words distorted as their mouths fill to the brim. Excuse me, what did you say? *I love you.* That's what I thought. I'm on to it, of course, the mirage, the sandwich turning to sand in my mouth, but it feels so good to be full again. I close my eyes altogether, gorge myself, like a sea creature who feasts on plastic to satisfy their hunger and is left with a gut full of want, emptier than ever.

Into the Woods

I. I can explain

Maybe the witch wasn't a witch at all, not to start with at least. She was just a mother who couldn't feed her babies (a missing father, a bad harvest), who watched them wilt, empty stomachs hard and bulbous from want, who never used it as an excuse to banish them to the forest one day, who stewed all the dandelion greens she could find until the earth around her for a mile was barren. Maybe some well-meaning woman came and took her children to someone who could properly provide for them, and the witch who wasn't yet a witch lost it, begged for death, downed what should have been enough poisonous mushrooms to do her in, sliced deep into her arms her children's initials (funny enough also h and g), and cruelly couldn't die. To add insult to injury, the mushroom overdose gave her the power to magically transform anything into food; she could touch the earth and watch it become shortbread, turn the siding to streusel, her roof to treacle tarts. Now that she had no mouths to feed, she had infinite bread. When the children wandered in she was delusional, thought they were hers finally returning to her, fattened Hansel in the cage so he could never leave again, and yes, she can't deny she put him in the oven, but in her defense she put all her dearest possessions in the oven these days to keep them warm and safe: family photos, dentures, her ax, her baby boy at long last returned to her.

II. An oven, a high tower, a wolf's stomach

What if the mother, portrayed as a heartless hag, actually grounded them to the outside because she thought they'd be better off with the witches and the wolves? This way they wouldn't see their mother and her companions quibble over the quantity of cocaine each got, their faces wan in the low light as they watch it bubble on the spoon; this way they wouldn't witness the adults hallucinate maggots on the carpet, run around the room pulling at their hair, and finally decide to pour bleach on the imaginary squirming mass; they wouldn't observe them afterward when they are flaccid taffy in the sun, goo people, terrifyingly unsolid. The girl had seen it before, so while he complained it was cold and he was hungry, bemoaned the unfairness of being left to wander the woods, wondered what they were doing back in the cottage, she took their exile as the gift it was. She knew first-hand that an oven, a high tower, a wolf's stomach, a vulture pulling at what is left, anything was better than seeing their mother like that.

III. Archetypes

In most fairy tales there's a kind, gullible father stripped of his reason by a temptress of a new wife. He is off chopping wood, trying and failing to make ends meet, surely not abandoning his children. But where I come from, there were no fathers, all good intentions and sweaty brows, no witches either, not really. It was just mothers and children and we all took turns playing those two roles; sometimes we would make the mac 'n' cheese with tuna, bring it to her where she slept all day, and get excited later when we found an empty plate that meant she had been awake and eaten what we made. Or sometimes when she went off into the forest for days and we prayed she would find her way back to us, we mothered each other, swaddled the baby in whatever scraps we could find, huddled around the TV at night like a fire. And sometimes we would play it the regular way, with her as the clear-eyed caretaker, wiping our brows, tucking us in, whispering a fairy tale to help us drift off to sleep.

IV. What hunger makes you do

When resources are scarce, when there isn't enough white bread or sandwich meat, or ho hos, or praise, or shoes, and you are often grounded to the outside and wander all day in the forest hungry and bored, the witch is you: you will put one another in the oven, not to eat your brother, and not even because you are logical enough to know without them you might get more, and not because it heals your pain (you know it doesn't). You do it because there is some empty space in you left by want, a pockmark where something good used to be or never grew in the first place, and it whispers to you "demolish them," "how fucking dare they look at you like that." You must grind them into little pieces with words and fists and betrayals. So you baste them, stuff the apple in their mouth, and slam the oven door. But when you smell the flesh start to turn to meat, guilt seizes you: you pull them out, blow on their singed hair, castigate your old self, realize they are all you have, hug them tight, ugly cry, ask what came over you? And then, like a dance, you switch leads and do it all again. Finally, because the sun is setting and you understand what it is to be hungry in all ways and would never squander breadcrumbs like those in the original tale, you use each other as guides to make your way back to whatever passes for home.

V. Fattened up

So, it was sort-of like turning straw into gold, but there was no troll. Just food stamps and Walmart, and with extreme couponing a few dollars could blossom into almost infinite foodstuffs: hydrogenated, corn-syruped, artificially-flavored, available in spicy inferno, ranch, and cinnamon churro. And there was still an impossible trade off, not a whole baby but parts of all of them in a way. She knew this miracle food was one part poison from quickly scanning the terms and conditions of the bargain, had been given the prediabetic warning at the doctor for her nine-year old whose neck was several shades darker than the rest of his body, an insulin resistant noose tightening all the time, a sign that he might soon like her need daily injections, but the alternative was nothing, was starvation, was going to school and telling the social worker they couldn't concentrate because they were hungry. And with the magical neverending-gingerbread-house food she got to witness them sated over and over, watch them close their eyes with pleasure at the joy of being filled all the way up by someone who loves them. And if in the end that is what kills them, so much pleasure and filling and knowing your mother's doing right by you, then what a way to go?

Tapestry

In fourth grade, my mother sold her food stamps to pay my gifted camp tuition. The man we lived with that year, (who sometimes kept her captive in his room all day), squeezed her thigh and told her how she would make up the money as he drove us to the far away college where I would stay in a dorm and learn ancient Greek. Until the day she died, she bragged that her 4th grader went to college. It was part of her origin story. Like the time in second grade she got me Capezio shoes and a dress from Marshall Fields, which I wore for two years of seismic growth until my breast buds burst against the worn nearly sheer fabric, until it went from mid calf to mid thigh. The shoes were fortunately lost in our transience or I would have had to wedge my feet in them, buckled and bloody to prove we were worth something. The dress was a thread she wove into conversations 20 years later, what it cost, sixty dollars, how beautiful I looked in it, don't ask how she got the money. In high school, she paid for my converse in installments at an interest rate that should have been illegal because I cried when she suggested the kmart version. Sometimes the electric was off, the gas, we skipped meals, but she made sure I had at least something. She wove these stories in the evenings, in the car when she was at her wits end, under her breath, chanted them like a mantra, until they were thick like an irish sweater, bearing the sacrifices she made in its knots and twists, its dropped stitches. Those sweaters were designed to identify the bodies of sailors when the flesh was too far gone, the wool knit surviving the carnivorous sea creatures, the bacteria, the bloat, so you knew that the bearer came from somewhere, from someone who loved them enough to craft this fine thing. Her tapestry kept her warm, insulated her from want. And when I was grown and owned a home and had a husband and dental insurance and a job where I got to wear dress up clothes everyday, and she was still struggling to make the ends meet, her rotting teeth so painful to get treatment in the ER, or maybe just some real painkillers to take the edge off, she contemplated crashing her car. She held her story garment close, snuggled it against her chest, breathed in its must like a soccer mom smelling laundry in a fabric softener commercial. I was surprised they didn't describe it on the autopsy when she died at only 59, murdered mostly by the gulf between what she had and what she needed. They detailed what was left of her clothes, just one flowered sock washed almost patternless, cotton underwear, but the tapestry that told the story of how she fertilized the earth with her own bones was nowhere to be found, so I reknit this replica, pull it around me, huff it to remind myself that I come from someone who cared enough to craft me this fine thing.

Like Demeter

my mother's father locked the corn flakes in the trunk of his car and decided when the hungry deserved to be fed. He doled out measured scoops each morning, said he didn't trust my grandmother not to overindulge the children. In truth, he wanted to throttle the fountain of calories like a God, to keep them all obedient, in line, while he, more like Zeus specifically, treated his girlfriend to furs, nights on the town. He knew my grandmother would do anything to keep her children fed, keep the cornflakes and tinned ravioli flowing from the locked trunk, would endure the calls where if he didn't answer the girlfriend hung up, which evolved to the boldness of just asking for him no matter who answered, and in the end, it was the mistress that demanded the divorce. My mother told me this story the night the cops came. My stepfather was weary of my smart mouth. He demanded I not eat the rice krispies he paid for, which resulted in me pouring myself a bowl anyway, him trying to wrench the box from hands, me curled around it like a lovey, then a scuffle, a headlock, me biting his forearm for release. When the cops arrived they saw my stepfather, shirt torn away from the collar, unable to make eye contact. They saw me 12 wearing a not long enough t-shirt, mascara fleeing down my face. They saw the spray of cereal on the ground where it landed after flying from the box in a perfect arc when I refused to let go, because, in fact, I paid for them with my babysitting money, which I secreted away in a glass rabbit. They saw my mother sobbing, tears streaming even from her nose. She kept muttering she swore she would never let this happen to her children, but like Persephone there was a bait and switch, somehow like her own mother she was lured by the promise of plenty. Then, as long as the cornflakes arrive on schedule to live with yourself you say *I do so like pomegranates; Hades is not that bad when you get to know him.*

Cut

You read how in sieged cities hungry people gnaw wood, boil leather, hallucinate. So it makes sense when your children's emptiness makes you crazed, unsteady, makes you line the inside of your shirt with whatever fits, flat things are best: kool-aid packets, boiled ham warm against your skin, tortillas in the breast pocket of the coat you are wearing despite the heat, but this is how you learned to do it when it was still winter, when you first had the idea, when they were crying all the time with the watered-down oatmeal you were making stretch until you got your stamps, and you thought why don't I just take it? But now it's July, and everyone is staring and a package of ramen leaks out the bottom hem and the cashier gives you that look like goddammit-I-don't get-paid-enough-for-this. And then you are in the back room with the cameras that watch everybody, when the manager says he is going to call the police or else maybe there is some way you can make it up to him, tells you to take off your top so he can see what else you have and the American-cheese slices and squeeze bottle of jelly spill forth from your bra and the cold plastic packaging leaves red impressions on your skin, which you try to focus on while he is taking his "cut," his words, and you left them both of them in front of the TV and you've got to get back and the milk, could he throw that in too? If there is anything else you can do to help him with his "cut," because using this code is doing something exciting for him like a wig might for another man. You keep counting up the thin, dense food, now strewn about his desk. You are making calculations: how much more could you get and what is the calorie-per-minute ratio and will it be enough? It's never enough. But it will work for now and with the stamps you will try to get the filling stuff, cheap, lots of it, white bread like pillow stuffing, boxed macaroni, snack cakes, the stuff that really works and you will fill them to bursting, watch the luster come back, feel the pride knowing you did your job, and it's a trade-off, yes, but everyone works to eat. And it's worth it because when they're hungry, they're different. You've seen it sometimes, they turn on each other when they think one has had more, like your childhood chameleons, how one ate the other while you were gone, and afterward just sat sunning on its rock like nothing happened. So you try all the stores, and sometimes get caught on purpose if you're onto the boss being a man, and you know the trick is when he asks what else you've got, you give him a little show, and usually they go for it, and if they don't, they at least never call the cops and they give you whatever you've soiled with the warmth of your body.

ROI

In any new venture there is sacrifice: His belly sits like a bowling ball on top of his belt buckle; what little hair he has is always wet with grease. He smells like your father's friends and acts like them too, the way they used to get too close, wink and smile when the other adults left the room. You met him right after tax returns, so you bought the tube top, the perfume, the heels. This is not frivolous spending but investment capital. You understand this because you studied economics briefly before *your kids* came along and the first husband left and the good boyfriend got cancer. If you pretend you don't have *them* a little bit, loiter at bingo as if you're in no hurry, maybe he'll forget what he said about not wanting to take on someone else's mess and invite you all to come live in his palace, with the hot water and full pantry, instead of the unheated apartment, where you pray that they fall seamlessly asleep behind the locked door, that the VHS tapes you use to entertain them in your absence, which skip and stutter in places from repeated play, don't break. And finally, just like you planned, when you say you have to get back to *them* at a pivotal moment, he asks why don't you just bring them here, there's plenty of room. Then you're all in the palace, and it's as lovely as you imagined, especially when he's at work and it's all yours: a fairy tale of bright light and fabric softener and matching plates piled high, and in this new setting *they* are bathed and pink and fleshy and laughing, and you tuck them in like a sitcom. But when he's home there's a list of demands. You must service him, keep earning it. When he says it's time *they learned some discipline*, especially the older girl with her defiant gaze that tells him she knows everything, you have a plan. He's only home and awake for so many hours. He works 2nd shift, so in the summers you pack them a lunch and make them stay out all day. *It's an adventure*, you tell them when you pull the covers from their sleeping bodies. While they're gone, you give him what he has paid for, allow him to sweat over you while he makes you tell him how you're all his. For the hundredth time, the bile rises in your throat, so you try to focus on a point in the distance to get through it, and as you always do, you run the cost benefit analysis. You realize you may already be in the stage of diminishing returns, consider if you can disinvest, if he'll follow you, and even though you know about the sunk cost fallacy, you really feel you've already given up so much, how can you afford to stop now?

Prepper

She had been through lean times, (I mean when weren't they?) but she means when there really wasn't enough to fill the cavities in their bellies: when she watched them fight over crackers, for dinner once prepared a box of Jiffy muffin mix with nothing but water and split the rubbery yield among 5, garbage picked the contents of a gas station dumpster after a fire made everything technically unsellable, wept when her children reported they did not eat their free school lunch. It is a mother's job to feed her children, and when you can't, something breaks in you, your mind is a frenzy always hustling to turn nothing into calories, bulk, something to chew. So later, when the foreclosure notice came/the light bill was unpayable/ the children now grown with full bellies struggled to work/live, she protected them the only way she knew, gathering food from dollar stores and food pantries like a magpie on speed: cans of potted meat, boxes of tuna helper, obscure jarred frostings, all past their sell by date. Much of it was boxes of dust: dehydrated corn syrup ground to sparkly flint, gelatin, stabilizers, MSG, flecks of green. When reconstituted with water it transforms to the equivalent of stacking all the furniture against the door. She fashioned her stores into fortress walls, flanks of soldiers, a watch tower, a moat, stocked all the cabinets, a storage room, an extra freezer, every pocket of space filled with insurance that it won't come to that again. In the end, there was enough to eat, but everybody was hungry for something else: affection, work, revenge, alcohol, some of it surely grounded in that earlier time of want, but there is no feeding it now, the statute of limitations is long past. Afterwards, her cupboards remained full. She could never bring herself to throw it out—it was a keepsake, a relic, a historic fortress made of highly-processed corn, long covered in moss, trees growing on the inside, useless, but still proof of how hard she tried to cushion them from want, how she did her job, just look.

Fruitful

"Your children will be kings"—The witches, *Macbeth*

They tell you to be fruitful and multiply, but nobody talks about what it means to be the fruit: that your flesh provides for the seed, either by tempting an animal into devouring and excreting it somewhere it might take root or the seed's pulpy flesh becoming the offspring's first meal. Like the pseudoscorpian mother, who if she fails to find her babies food, exposes her juicy joints to allow them to suck her dry. Or like when my mother, before she died a month after her 59th birthday, her arteries waxing full of stress and eating the leavings, refused to buy or prepare herself special food, ate last, when it was cold, sometimes once every 24 hours when the starvation pain hits, and in between just alternated candy and insulin while she filled everyone else. Mothers offer themselves for desiccation and end up husks, sucked so dry they are unrecognizable; all so their children might root somewhere where conditions are ripe for life. So many children have been planted in more auspicious soil, with a kiss on the forehead and a demand to *stay right here* while the parents make themselves into fertilizer—because as the witches knew when they taunted Macbeth, the only thing better than taking it for yourself, is giving the crown to your children: firmly rooted, dewy, swollen or at the very least full of as much fruit flesh as you can manage.

Sight

She needed a break from seeing it: the one daughter's drinking, the one daughter breaking her hand on the other daughter's face, the vodka-filled water bottles, the strategically placed puke buckets, the grandbaby turning his sleeping mother over on her side like he had been taught, etc., etc. So she squirreled away a few dollars to stay at a cheap hotel. She felt guilty about leaving them, but also if she didn't remove herself she would do something dangerous. She couldn't see it anymore, couldn't see her baby she made with her body asleep in the snow. Well, technically, she didn't see that, the police just described it to her, but you get my drift. She was watching her creation destroy herself and there was nothing she could do, (believe me she tried all the things) but watch because she didn't have the heart to do what the books said and put her baby out on the street. What she really wanted out of the hotel was the hot tub, to close her eyes in, to shut down completely in. And she did ease her body into the almost painful water, and it did feel so good, the temporary reprieve, the halo of steam obscuring her sight, but lurking in the water was a single-celled organism which squirmed into her eye. It was a desperate grasp at relief, both her plunge and the parasite's. It curled itself under the doorway of her eyelid, embedded itself in the fleshy tissue, and started feasting. She came home with one eye shut. Disoriented. Nothing was better. The one daughter was unconscious in a grocery store bathroom. And the doctors couldn't figure the eye out. At first, they thought it was a trauma, then a bacterial infection until an eye specialist determined that, no, that's a living thing in your cornea, preparing for its departure to your central nervous system. It was painful, an anvil in her skull, but the closed eye wasn't empty. Instead, it offered a different vision. In it, she saw her daughter sober, happy, apple-cheeked, riding a fucking horse, lisa-frank style, walking down an aisle, white dress, a trail of babies, so clean. In the other open, still-operational eye, the daughter is running up a hill mostly naked, it is cold out, she is warning the neighbors about hallucinated phantoms. The mother wanted to close both eyes, to give up, and if the medicine didn't work, she'd die with her happy baby on the backs of her eyelids. And this is how she figures the light works, the one you walk toward, the glowing embrace that protects us, the calming fiction that gives mothers permission to let go, to pretend it's all going to be okay: they can fend for themselves now, no need to be there to turn them on their side.

Plenty

Like jesus with the loaves and fishes and the wine, she is trying to perform miracles of plenty. She brings them in from the cold, dozens of them. They are shoulder to shoulder in the living room, sandwiched like cigarettes in a fresh pack. The number is always growing. She can't bear to see any living thing outside, exposed, unmothered. But once inside, the newly-mothered, at first relieved, perceive another danger. Every flat surface is a bed, and some are sleeping back-to-back or in shifts. Even respiration is a problem at this scale, the air heavy with carbon dioxide from the exhaling of sighs and cigarettes. Even after they are fed, their faces are taught, still bent to her, begging for more. They try to elbow each other out for an extra ration of something more than food, but the squirming makes them seem more uniform, not less, a writhing mass, an organ, pulsing with unmet want. It's the same way the plants in my garden battle for sunlight. Each one extends its tendrils as far as possible toward the light, desperate to come out on top of the dogpile of woven leaves and shoots. A good gardener culls, thins, engineers the space so each surviving plant can access the nourishment it needs, each can stretch its phalanges wide like hands with palms open to the sun. If not, if you are too soft to pick the winners and losers, if you become distracted and allow nature to take its course, there is a fight for dominance. Their leaves jut each way, too densely packed. Instead of being able to bathe outspread in the light, their cramped leaves are forced to fold like hands clasped in prayer, pleading to the sky.

Acknowledgments

I sincerely thank the following publications in which these pieces previously appeared, sometimes in slightly different versions.

5 X 5: "Infestation"

Agni: "Cut"

Blood Tree Review: "Teeth," "Changeling," "Grandmother," "Bargain,"

BODY: "I can explain"

Compressed Journal of Creative Arts: "Short Shorts"

Driftwood Press Anthology 2024: "Cry it out"

Five South: "Adaptation"

Gone Lawn: "The mothers," "plenty"

Harpy Hybrid Review: "The disappearing mothers of Victorian baby photography," "Offerings"

Howling Mad Review: "Persephone"

Passages North: "Surrogate," "Tethered"

Pithead Chapel: "The bends"

Posit: "Sight," "Prepper," "the pull of the water"

South Carolina Review: "What hunger Makes you do," "An oven, a high tower, a wolf's stomach," "Archetypes," "On contingency plans when one cannot release one's young into the wild"

The Racket: Genesis Suite (published as Nursing Suite), Family Tree Suite

Vestal Review "ROI"

Women's Studies Quarterly: "Unraveling" (Published as "Barren") "Unraveling" also appeared as "Barren" in my chapbook *The Tyranny of Heirlooms*, Sundress Publications, 2018.

With deep appreciation to Daniel Borzutzky, Mark Donahue, Will Ejzak, Peter Kahn, Laura Young, and Glynis Kinnan for the generous gift of their time spent offering feedback on these poems.

www.ingramcontent.com/pod-product-compliance
Lightning Source LLC
Chambersburg PA
CBHW030059170426
43197CB00010B/1589